How It Is Made

Peanuts to Peanut Butter

B.J. Best

Cavendish
Square

New York

RAP   3 2401 00903 897 9

Published in 2017 by Cavendish Square Publishing, LLC
243 5th Avenue, Suite 136, New York, NY 10016

First Edition

CPSIA Compliance Information: Batch #CW17CSQ

All websites were available and accurate when this book was sent to press.

Library of Congress Cataloging-in-Publication Data

Names: Best, B.J.
Title: Peanuts to peanut butter / B.J. Best.
Description: New York : Cavendish Square Publishing, 2017. | Series: How it is made | Includes index.
Identifiers: ISBN 9781502621344 (pbk.) | ISBN 9781502621368 (library bound) |
ISBN 9781502621351 (6 pack) | ISBN 9781502621375 (ebook)
Subjects: LCSH: Peanut butter--Juvenile literature. | Peanuts--Processing--Juvenile literature.
Classification: LCC TP438.P4 B47 2017 | DDC 641.3'56596--dc23

Editorial Director: David McNamara
Copy Editor: Rebecca Rohan
Associate Art Director: Amy Greenan
Designer: Alan Sliwinski
Production Coordinator: Karol Szymczuk
Photo Research: J8 Media

The photographs in this book are used by permission and through the courtesy of: Cover Stephen Mcsweeney/Shutterstock (right); Cover IVL/Shutterstock (left); p. 5 IS_ImageSource/IStockPhoto; p. 7 wilaiwan jantra/Shutterstock; p. 9 Inga Spence/Getty Images Entertainment/Getty Images; p. 11 Larrie Chue /EyeEm/Getty Images Entertainment/Getty Images; p. 13 Michael C. Gray/ Shutterstock; p. 15 Joy Skipper/Getty Images Entertainment/Getty Images; p. 17 Maren Caruso/Getty Images Entertainment/Getty Images; p. 19 Mark Waugh/Alamy Stock Photo; p. 21 JupiterImages/Getty Images Entertainment/Getty Images.

Printed in the United States of America

Contents

Peanut butter is a popular snack.

It is healthy.

It tastes good!

5

Peanuts aren't nuts.

They are **legumes**, like peas or beans.

They grow underground.

Peanuts are **harvested**.

They are cleaned.

Their shells are removed.

9

The peanuts are **roasted**.

They are heated and cooked.

11

The skins on the peanuts are removed.

This is called **blanching**.

It makes peanuts a lighter color.

13 ⭐

The peanuts are **ground**.

They become a thick paste.

15

Oil, sugar, and salt
are added.

The peanut butter is mixed.

17

The peanut butter is ready!

It is put in jars.

It is shipped to stores.

You can make peanut butter at home.

You need a blender.

Ask an adult to help!

21

New Words

blanching (BLAN-ching) Making a lighter color.

ground (GROUND) Crushed into small pieces.

harvested (HAR-vist-ed) Collected a crop.

legumes (lih-GYOOMS) Plants that grow fruit in pods or shells.

roasted (ROH-sted) Cooked with heat.

Index

23

About the Author

B.J. Best lives in Wisconsin with his wife and son. He has written several other books for children. He likes peanut butter and chocolate together.

About

Bookworms help independent readers gain reading confidence through high-frequency words, simple sentences, and strong picture/text support. Each book explores a concept that helps children relate what they read to the world they live in.